This book belongs to

....

It was given to me by

....

On this date

....

RUTH & ME

Devotions for Girls

Trisha
White Priebe

BARBOUR kidz
A Division of Barbour Publishing

To Avy and Willow

Your mom was the reason I first learned to love the life of Ruth. Ask her to sing the song.

© 2025 by Barbour Publishing, Inc.

ISBN 979-8-89151-123-1

All rights reserved. No part of this publication may be reproduced or transmitted for commercial purposes, except for brief quotations in printed reviews, without written permission of the publisher. Reproduced text may not be used on the World Wide Web. No Barbour Publishing content may be used as artificial intelligence training data for machine learning, or in any similar software development.

Churches and other noncommercial interests may reproduce portions of this book without the express written permission of Barbour Publishing, provided that the text does not exceed 500 words and that the text is not material quoted from another publisher. When reproducing text from this book, include the following credit line: "From *Ruth & Me Devotions for Girls*, published by Barbour Publishing, Inc. Used by permission."

Unless otherwise noted, all scripture quotations are taken from the New Life™ Version, copyright © 1969 and 2003 by Barbour Publishing, Inc., Uhrichsville, Ohio 44683. All rights reserved.

Scripture quotations marked SKJV are taken from the Barbour Simplified KJV™ Bible, copyright © 2022 by Barbour Publishing, Inc., Uhrichsville, Ohio 44683. All rights reserved.

Cover illustrations by Pedro Riquelme

Published by Barbour Publishing, Inc., 1810 Barbour Drive, Uhrichsville, Ohio 44683, www.barbourbooks.com

Our mission is to inspire the world with the life-changing message of the Bible.

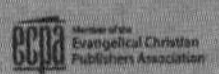

Printed in China.

002480 0525 DS

Welcome to

Ruth & Me

Devotions for Girls!

Meet Ruth—a woman whose courage and faithfulness set her apart in the Bible and made her name one to remember.

This story is filled with love, hope, and the extraordinary strength found in the heart of a woman chosen by God to play an important role in His plan of salvation.

With each exciting chapter of her life, you will discover how God had a special purpose for Ruth, guiding her steps and weaving her story into His larger plan. Just as Ruth trusted in God's leading, you too can find courage and faith to fulfill your own unique role in God's grand design.

Let Ruth's example inspire you to trust God's direction. And let her help you to believe that you can make a lasting impact on those around you for God's glory.

FOREIGN
GIRL

A DARK TIME

In the days when there were judges to rule, there was a time of no food in the land.

RUTH 1:1

You hold in your hands a love story.

In these pages, you'll see how a woman named Ruth showed great kindness, loyalty, and faith. You'll also learn how love changed her story and yours.

But before you meet her, you need to know how her story began.

A time long ago, judges ruled the land. God's people had stopped trusting and obeying Him in the way they had been taught to.

It was a dark and sad time in Israel's history.

Then—to make matters worse—there was a famine in the country. During a famine, there is not enough food for everyone to eat. Many people go hungry and get very sick. It caused trouble in Bethlehem, a town in Judah.

A man named Elimelech lived in Bethlehem with his wife, Naomi, and their two sons. Struggling to survive the famine, they decided to pack up their belongings and move far away to another country, called Moab.

But what does any of this have to do with Ruth?

Let's see what happens next.

God, thank You for putting Ruth's story in the Bible so I can read and learn from it. Thank You for helping me during every dark or scary time in my life. Amen.

A NEW HOME

They went into the land of
Moab and stayed there.

Ruth 1:2

The journey to Moab was long and difficult.

Elimelech and his family walked many miles, crossing hills and valleys, always looking for a place where they could find food and safety. When they finally reached Moab, they settled down and started a new life in their new home.

Unfortunately, Moab was a place where people worshiped idols—false gods and statues—instead of the true and living God. In fact, Moab was considered an enemy of Israel, God's people.

It was important to Elimelech and Naomi that their two sons should grow up and marry women who loved God—not foreign women who worshiped idols.

But then something terrible happened. Elimelech died, leaving Naomi alone with their two sons in this strange land.

And in the very next part of the story, the two sons "married Moabite women. The name of one was Orpah. The name of the other was Ruth" (Ruth 1:4).

So, who was this foreign girl named Ruth, who worshiped idols?

Let's keep reading.

God, thank You that when everything looks hopeless, You are still good. Help me to remember I can always hope and trust in You. Amen.

A TERRIBLE LOSS

Both Mahlon and Chilion died.
Naomi was left without her two
children and her husband.

Ruth 1:5

Just when you hope the story will get better, things take one more bad turn. Both of Naomi's sons died, leaving Naomi all alone in the world.

But was Naomi really alone? No, God was always with Naomi, just as He is always with you.

While we don't know how Naomi's sons died, we know that everything in Naomi's life must have felt like it was spinning out of control.

First, she lost her home in Bethlehem.

Then she lost her husband.

Finally, she lost her sons.Naomi's heart must have felt as if it were breaking in a thousand pieces.

In time, she would have to learn a hard but good truth: that even when things felt really bad, God was still there, ready to comfort and help her through any challenges.

The same is true for you. No matter how difficult life may seem, God's love and care are always there to support and guide you.

Let's see if this story gets any better.

God, just as You were always
with Naomi, You are always
with me. Help me to trust
that You are always close
when I need You. Amen.

A HUGE DECISION

But Naomi said to her two daughters-in-law, "Go, each one of you return to your own mother's house. May the Lord show kindness to you, as you have done with the dead and with me."

RUTH 1:8

Finally, Naomi received some good news.

She learned that the famine back in Bethlehem had come to an end, and “the Lord had brought food to His people” (Ruth 1:6). This meant that there would be food and hope again.

So, Naomi made plans to return to her homeland.

But she also made a plan to leave behind her daughters-in-law, Orpah and Ruth. She knew it would be hard for them to be young widows in a foreign land, so she encouraged them both to stay in Moab with their parents. She told them she was praying that they would be able to find love and get married again.

But Orpah and Ruth did not like what Naomi had to say. The Bible says they cried in loud voices. And they both knew they had a huge decision to make—to go with Naomi back to Bethlehem or to stay with family in Moab.

Orpah chose to stay in Moab.

Ruth, on the other hand, had another idea in mind.

Lord God, when I have a big decision to make, please give me Your wisdom—and the courage to do what You say.

YOUNG
WIDOW

A LOVING PROMISE

"I will go where you go. I will live where you live. Your people will be my people. And your God will be my God."

RUTH 1:16

Naomi tried hard to convince Ruth to stay in Moab with her family. But Ruth refused.

Instead, Ruth said, "Do not beg me to leave you or turn away from following you. I will go where you go. I will live where you live. Your people will be my people. And your God will be my God. I will die where you die, and there I will be buried" (Ruth 1:16–17).

Ruth's words showed deep love and loyalty. She promised to stay with Naomi no matter what happened. When Naomi saw that Ruth was determined to stay, she said no more.

Together, they would travel back to Bethlehem to see what plans God had for their lives.

Staying loyal to people is one way we show love. How can you show loyalty to your family and friends during difficult times?

Thankfully, this isn't the end of the story for Naomi and Ruth. In some ways, it is just the beginning! Let's see what happens next.

God, thank You for Ruth's example of being loyal and loving to Naomi. Please help me to be loyal and loving to You and to the friends and family You've given me. Amen.

A CHANGED NAME

She said to them, "Do not call me Naomi.
Call me Mara. For the All-powerful
has brought much trouble to me."

Ruth 1:20

Ruth and Naomi traveled together until they finally reached Bethlehem.

As they walked through the town, people began to notice them. In fact, the Bible says, "The whole town of Bethlehem was happy because of them" (Ruth 1:19). And the women in the town began to ask, "Is this Naomi?"

But Naomi was very sad. She had lost her husband and two sons in Moab. Her life had become much more difficult than when she left Bethlehem to live in Moab.

So, Naomi said to the townspeople, "Do not call me Naomi. Call me Mara. For the

All-powerful has brought much trouble to me."

In the Bible, the name *Mara* means "bitter." Naomi was so sad about her life that she didn't even want to be called by her real name.

But even during this difficult time, Ruth faithfully loved Naomi and stayed by her side.

Neither of these women could imagine the wonderful plans God had for their future.

What happened next was truly amazing.

God, I know that even when it looks as if things are going wrong, You are still in control. I can trust You. Amen.

A HARD WORKER

So Ruth went and gathered in the field behind those who picked the grain.

RUTH 2:3

After returning to Bethlehem, Ruth and Naomi needed to find food to eat.

But there were no grocery stores. And even if there had been stores like we know, Ruth and Naomi had very little money.

In those days, poor people and widows would gather leftover grain in other people's fields after the harvesters had finished their work. This was called gleaning. It was a way God's people helped those in need.

Ruth wanted to take care of Naomi. So, she said to Naomi one morning, "Let me go to the field to gather grain behind someone who might show favor to me" (Ruth 2:2).

Naomi agreed.

Ruth's willingness to work in the fields showed her love for and loyalty to Naomi.

Each day, Ruth probably went out early in the morning to work hard in the fields, picking up the leftover grain. Her hard work and dedication showed her strong character and her deep care for Naomi.

In what ways do you work hard to show your love for others?

God, please help me to work hard, just as Ruth did. Give me the strength and energy to do my best each day. Amen.

A KIND STRANGER

And she happened to come to the part of the field that belonged to Boaz, who was of the family of Elimelech.

Ruth 2:3

As she worked, Ruth came to a part of the field that belonged to Boaz, a kind and generous man.

Boaz noticed Ruth working hard in the field and asked his workers about her. When he learned who she was and how she was taking care of Naomi, Boaz admired her. In fact, Boaz told his workers to leave extra grain on purpose for Ruth to gather. He wanted to make sure she was always safe.

Ruth took plenty of grain to Naomi, filling their home with food and hope.

After so much sadness, God was making a way. God was showing His kindness through Boaz's generosity.

In what ways has God shown His kindness to you through the people in your life? Who has been loving or helpful to you?

Ruth's hard work and faithfulness were being rewarded, and Naomi could see that brighter days were ahead.

But neither Ruth nor Naomi could have imagined what would happen next. What do you think happens next in the story?

God, thank You for always making a way, even when I can't yet see what it is. Amen.

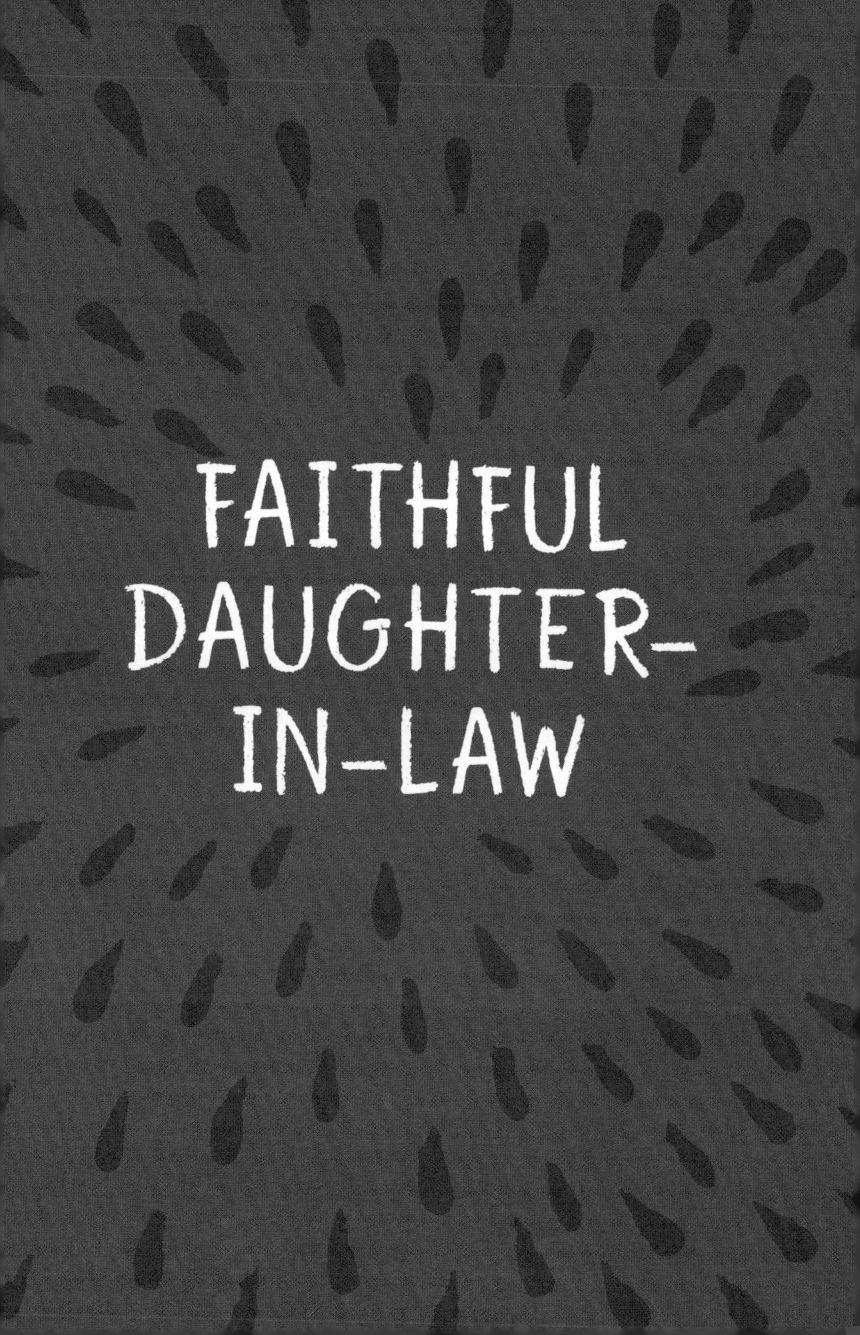
FAITHFUL
DAUGHTER-
IN-LAW

A GOOD REPUTATION

Boaz said to her, "I have heard about all you have done for your mother-in-law after the death of your husband."

RUTH 2:11

Ruth continued working hard in Boaz's field, gathering grain to take home to Naomi.

One day, Boaz approached Ruth and spoke kindly to her. Ruth was humbled, so she asked him, "Why do you care about me? I am a stranger from another land." Boaz answered, "I have heard about all you have done for your mother-in-law after the death of your husband. I have heard how you left your father and mother and the land of your birth to come to a people you did not know before" (Ruth 2:10–11).

Boaz knew about Ruth's loyalty to Naomi.

Ruth had a very good reputation, which means people like Boaz thought highly of her because of her good actions and character. Ruth's love for her mother-in-law changed Naomi's life. But it would also change Ruth's life.

Do you have a reputation for loving others and being kind?

Ruth didn't understand how everything was about to change, but it would all become clear soon enough.

Let's keep reading.

God, please give me strength to do my best in everything I do, so that I can be known for doing what is right. Amen.

Ruth said to her,
"I will do all that you say."

RUTH 3:5

One day, Naomi had an idea.

She wanted to help Ruth find a good husband who would take care of her. Naomi knew that Boaz, the man who owned the fields where Ruth worked, was a good man.

So, Naomi gave Ruth special instructions. She told Ruth to clean up, put on her best clothes, and wait until nighttime to go to the threshing floor where Boaz worked.

Then Naomi gave Ruth a few more instructions that might sound a bit strange to us today. But they were a special way of asking Boaz for his protection and help. Naomi told Ruth she should tell Boaz that she needed him to help take care of her.

Can you imagine how nervous Ruth must have been?

Still, Ruth listened to Naomi's words.

She walked through the fields, the moonlight casting long shadows as she approached the threshing floor. As she stepped forward, her heart may have raced with hope and uncertainty.

But God gave Ruth courage to do what happened next.

God, help me always to listen
to the wise people in my
life who want to please You.
Even when the instructions
don't make sense to me,
help me to trust. Amen.

A GIANT RISK

So Ruth went down to the grain-floor and did all her mother-in-law had told her to do.

Ruth 3:6

It was a big risk for Ruth to go see Boaz at the threshing floor late at night.

In those days, it was unusual for a woman to go talk to a man the way Naomi told Ruth to talk to Boaz. Girls and women usually waited for men to talk to them first!

But Ruth loved Naomi, so she bravely followed Naomi's plan. She knew it was important to help her mother-in-law find a good future.

Because it was dark, Boaz asked, "Who are you?" Ruth answered, "I am Ruth." And she made her request. Boaz said, "Do not be afraid. I will do for you whatever you ask. For all my people in the city know that you are a good woman" (Ruth 3:9–11).

Ruth's risk worked out, because Boaz recognized her courage and promised his support. He promised to make sure that Ruth and Naomi would be safe.

But the people of Ruth's day had certain rules they lived by. There was still one important thing Boaz needed to do.

Everything would become clear soon enough.

God, please give me the courage to do the right thing even when it doesn't make sense to others. Amen.

A GOOD ANSWER

Boaz went up to the gate
and sat down there.

RUTH 4:1

Boaz needed to find an answer to one important question.

So, he went to the town gate where important decisions were made. He sat and waited until he found the man he needed to see.

According to the customs of this time—many of which are hard for us to understand today—a widow's closest relative had the first chance to marry her. And he could also buy her land.

Boaz found Naomi's closest relative. Then he gathered ten witnesses to listen to his words. He explained that Naomi was selling a piece of land that belonged to their family. But he also said that if the man bought the land, he would also have to marry Ruth.

The man thought about it. And Boaz probably felt a little nervous while he waited.

But in the end, the man decided not to buy the land or marry Ruth. He said that Boaz could buy the land and marry Ruth.

This was a good answer.

God, sometimes I worry about how things will turn out. Please help me to trust that all the details will come together in Your perfect way. Amen.

JOYFUL
MOTHER

A HAPPY DAY

The women said to Naomi,
"Thanks be to the Lord. He has not
left you without a family this day."

Ruth 4:14

Boaz and Ruth got married!

Do you love weddings? Because this wedding must have been an exciting one.

Boaz admired Ruth's kindness and courage, and Ruth was grateful for Boaz's protection and love. Living as widows had been hard for the women.

This wedding was a time of great joy and celebration, with friends and family gathered to share in their happiness.

Boaz and Ruth started a new life together. God's plan had come true, turning sadness into joy.

Their marriage was a beautiful example of how God can bring wonderful blessings out of difficult times.

But this wedding was also good news for Naomi, who was no longer alone—she had a loving family again. And she would be protected.

Remember earlier in the story when Naomi's heart felt like it was breaking in a thousand pieces? God was putting the pieces back together.

Naomi was once again a joyful mother.

God's plan had brought a new family together.

But this isn't the end of the story. God wasn't done adding to this special family.

God, thank You for writing the best stories for us. Please help me to trust Your plan for my life, just as Ruth and Naomi did. Amen.

A SPECIAL BABY

The Lord made it possible for her to have a child and she gave birth to a son.

RUTH 4:13

Exciting news spread throughout Bethlehem: Ruth had a baby boy!

Everyone celebrated because baby Obed was born. Ruth and Boaz thanked God for their precious son.

Did you know every baby is a gift from God? That's right! When you were born, you were a gift too. (And you still are!)

God was continuing to turn Ruth's sadness into happiness. Can you imagine how she must have gone from the deepest sadness to the greatest joy? Obed's arrival was a sweet reminder that God's plans are full of wonderful surprises and blessings.

The whole town rejoiced, knowing that Obed would grow up to be part of something amazing in God's big story. They told Naomi how excited they were about this child, saying, "Your daughter-in-law who loves you. . .has given birth to him" (Ruth 4:15).

But not even the town could imagine what would happen next. God has a way of doing better things than we can ask or imagine!

Every child, like Obed—and like you—is part of God's amazing plan.

God, thank You for doing wonderful things in my life. Help me to trust Your plan always. Amen.

A BIG DEAL

"You are happy because you believed.
Everything will happen as the
Lord told you it would happen."

RUTH 1:45

When Ruth gave birth to Obed, they became part of a very special family in God's big story.

Remember, Ruth wasn't originally from Bethlehem—she was from Moab. But she chose to stay with Naomi, even when it was hard. God saw Ruth's faithfulness and included her in His special plans.

Did you know that God can use anyone to do amazing things?

Obed was not just any baby. He would grow up to become the grandfather of King David, the most important king in Israel's history. And even more amazing, Jesus—God's own Son—was born into this family line.

Ruth's story reminds us that God's plans are always good, even when things seem hard or scary. At the beginning of Ruth's story, she was a Moabite woman who worshiped idols. But when she chose to trust Naomi's God—the true God—everything changed.

Obed's birth was part of God's bigger plan to bring Jesus into the world. He would save sinners and show us God's love!

God, thank You for bringing Jesus into the world. That is truly the greatest love story of all. Amen.

A GREAT EXAMPLE

The women said to Naomi,
"Thanks be to the Lord.
He has not left you without a
family this day. May his name
become known in all of Israel."

Ruth 4:14

So, how does the story of Ruth end?

The Bible doesn't say anything more about Ruth's life after the birth of her son, Obed. We don't know how long she lived or how many children God gave her. The book of Ruth ends with the genealogy—the special family tree showing how people are related to each other—linking Ruth to King David and, much later, to Jesus.

Ruth is one of only five women mentioned in the genealogy of Jesus found in the book of Matthew. What an honor!

Genealogies are like a map of our family history. They remind us that we are all part of a big story that God is writing with love and care.

What do you hope God is writing with the wonderful story of your life?

While details about Ruth's later life are not given to us in the Bible, we know she continues to be a great example of faith today.

What do you love most about Ruth?

God, thank You for Ruth's story and how she trusted You. Help me to be brave and faithful like she was. Thank You for loving me and for writing my story too. Amen.

WHY WE REMEMBER RUTH

A WOMAN OF LOYALTY

"So may the Lord do the same to me, and worse, if anything but death takes me from you."

RUTH 1:17

Though it's been thousands of years since Ruth lived on earth, she is still remembered for her remarkable loyalty.

Loyalty is one way we show that we care deeply about the people we love. When we're loyal to our friends, they know they can count on us to keep our word—which makes our bond even stronger.

Ruth's loyalty shines brightest in her relationship with her mother-in-law, Naomi. After the death of Ruth's husband, Ruth faced a choice: Stay in her homeland of Moab or follow Naomi back to Bethlehem.

As you know—in spite of the scary hardships that lay ahead—Ruth chose to stay with Naomi. She spoke the famous words, “Where you go, I will go, and where you lodge, I will lodge. Your people shall be my people, and your God my God” (Ruth 1:16 SKJV).

Ruth’s words were more than just a promise—they were a testimony to Ruth’s strong loyalty and deep love for Naomi.

Ruth kept her promise to Naomi. She was loyal.

God, please give me the strength to keep my promises and to be someone others can count on. Help me to be kind and helpful, just as You are to me. Amen.

A WOMAN OF DILIGENCE

"She said, 'Let me gather food behind the others who gather among the grain.' So she came and has stayed from morning until now."

RUTH 2:7

We remember Ruth for her loyalty. We also remember her for her diligence.

Diligence means working hard and staying focused on what you need to do, even when it's tough. It also means never stopping until the task is finished.

Whether you're cleaning your room, practicing an instrument, or helping a friend, being diligent means never giving up. Diligence shows others that you care about doing things well and that you can be trusted to finish what you start.

Ruth showed diligence by working hard in the fields to gather food for herself and Naomi. She didn't stop when she got tired, and she didn't quit because the job was difficult. She kept going because she knew it was important. Ruth's diligence was a demonstration of her love.

Though she was a poor widow in a foreign land, Ruth was diligent. Her hard work glorified God.

Ruth's diligence made a big difference in the lives of others—including Naomi's—and your diligence can make a difference too.

God, please help me to be diligent in everything I do. When I have schoolwork or chores, give me the strength to work hard and not give up. Help me to stay focused and do my best for You. Amen.

A WOMAN OF COURAGE

Ruth said to her,
"I will do all that you say."

Ruth 3:5

Ruth showed extraordinary courage throughout her story.

Her journey from Moab to Bethlehem, her dedication to Naomi, and her willingness to work a new job all demonstrate her bravery.

When Ruth went into the fields to glean leftover grain, she had to work alongside strangers. The decision to provide for Naomi in this way showed love, no matter how scary it must have been.

Courage means having a brave heart. It means making a good choice even if it feels hard or frightening. Being courageous doesn't mean you're never afraid—it means you try your best even when you're afraid.

We need courage for big things and for everyday things too. We need courage to try new things—like talking to a new girl at school or learning to ride a bike. We also need courage to stand up for what's right, especially when others don't agree.

God gave Ruth her courage, and He can give you courage too.

For so many reasons, we remember Ruth for her courage.

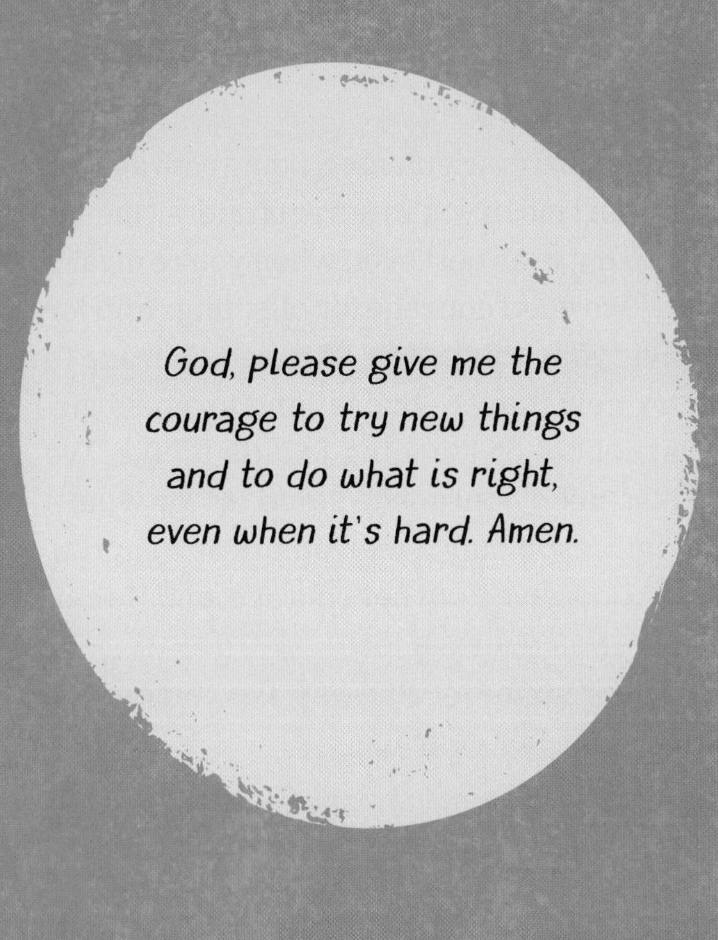

God, please give me the courage to try new things and to do what is right, even when it's hard. Amen.

A WOMAN OF LOVE

So Ruth. . .did all her
mother-in-law had told her to do.

Ruth 3:6

Yes, you hold in your hands a love story.

But not the type of love story found in fairy tales.

And not just the type of story where a man and woman fall in love—though Ruth did learn to love Boaz.

Ruth is a wonderful example of love in action. Her story shows how love should guide our decisions and help us care for others, even when it's not easy.

Ruth's story teaches us that love is more than just a feeling. It's about choosing to be kind, caring, and helpful to others, even when it's hard.

By the end of the story, Ruth's love extended to her new home. As a Moabite, Ruth was an outsider in Bethlehem, yet she joined Naomi's people and God wholeheartedly. Her willingness to adopt a new way of life out of respect for Naomi showed great love.

We remember Ruth because she was a woman of love.

Can you follow in Ruth's footsteps and be a young woman of love?

God, please help me to be a young woman known for her love. May my words and actions show kindness and compassion to everyone around me. Help me to love others just as You have loved me. Amen.